*Land
Diving*

Land Diving

New Poems by Robert Morgan

Louisiana State University Press

Baton Rouge   1976

Designer: Dwight Agner
Type face: VIP Trump Mediaeval
Typesetter: Graphic Composition, Inc., Athens, Georgia
Printer and binder: Moran Industries, Baton Rouge, Louisiana

Some of the poems in this volume have previously appeared in
the following publications, to which grateful acknowledgment
is made: *Apple, Brown's Window, Café Solo, Choice, Granite,
Lillabulero, New Directions 26, North Carolina Folklore Journal,
Poetry Now, Rapport, The Small Farm, Southern Poetry Review,
Southern Voices, The Stone,* and *Yale Review.*

LIBRARY OF CONGRESS CATALOGING IN PUBLICATION DATA

Morgan, Robert, 1944–
  Land diving.

  I. Title.
PS3563.O87147L3   811'.5'4   76–28168
ISBN 0–8071–0199–0
ISBN 0–8071–0274–1 pbk.

*For my
mother and father*

Contents

III   Paradise's Fool

Dark
Corner

I

Driven out from the centers of population,
displaced from villages and crossroads and too poor
to acquire the alluvial bottomlands,
the carbon-dark fields along the creek,

forced back on the rocky slopes above branches,
to the flanks near the headwaters,
pushed to the final mountain wall, I brace
my faculties against falling out of labor

and prop up or stake down every stalk, dig
terraces and drive fences to save what little
topsoil there is from the gullywashers
hitting almost every afternoon up here in summer.

Cow trails babel the steepest knobs, make
by spiral and switchback the sheer peaks
and outcroppings accessible. I plant only root
vegetables, turnips, potatoes, and prehensile creepers.

Too far to carry whole or raw things
into town, I take the trouble only with something
boiled down, distilled, and clear new
ground every three or four years.

I live high on the hogback near
dividing water, I disaffiliate and secede.
I grow ginseng in hollows unlit as the dark
side of the moon, and confederate with moisture and

insular height to bring summit orchards
to bear. I husband the scartissue of erosion.

Affliction

On the slopes where the old
blighted years ago,
new
chestnuts sprout and
thrive until the age of saplings, then
blossom and die.

How the old roots keep sending
shoots every spring
hoping the canker's gone.
How the buried sap must
remember the sun and
former height, keeping the veins

stoked winter after winter below
the frost-line, always raising a new stalk
like a periscope to find
if the poison has subsided, tasting
sweet wind off the
ridges and refueling on light,

after decades still trying to break through
and establish hold,
watching the new pumped by
hoarded sugars
and thrilled by the open
reach puberty, almost produce and

fertilize a seed before the curse
strikes the species back
into its dungeons.
Like us straining to ascend,
immortal
only in dirt.

I used to wonder how
two springs could issue from the hill
a yard apart. Why not dig deeper
and unite their flow?

And later realized they
surfaced close from opposite
directions. The southern
sweeter, though the northern's steady

effluence came cold, even in the dry
months when its neighbor
slacked and almost stood, with
algae thickening the edges.

In the church nearby I've heard
sermons on the trinity describe
their separate currents merging to
one branch. The sweet uneven

head rose from the hillside leaning toward
Dark Corner, while the constant
icy thread emerged
from the farm country. In summer

they condemned the slow one and
when I came down to drink before
or after preaching its partner sure
enough ran clear, with ebullition

dimpling the surface above the pores,
and purifying lizards gripped
the sandy floor. But after swilling
there I'd dip the gourd

into the slightly silty left
embellished now with leaves and spiders
and aquatic mosses for a richer sip.
That ungodly taste I'd carry home.

No fishing on Sunday
we crayoned on the plank above
the Lemmons Hole. At six or seven
I knew wetting a line then
would bait electric eels
that send underwater lighting
up the string
to kill the guilty angler
key or no.
The cowtrails came down into
the shallows of the pool
and for all I knew continued
to a fata morgana pasture of cocoons
below. Swimmers on the sabbath
would be taken by suckholes
and whirlpools down into
the sinks of filth.
Don't play with BB guns on
the Lord's Day or a pellet will
ricochet into an eyeball.
You follow a girl into the brush
along the creek after church
a cloudburst may wash
you out still coupled and naked
onto the sandbar
where they have baptizings.
Trash backs into the central
eddy and queues like a mocassin
coiling where the Cochran boy went down.
Current galls on rocks around the bend
where they found Grover
frozen with his bottle.

Sure I've seen kids walk to school
barefoot in the snow and stop
to warm their feet in the branch.
But every year the first of May
regardless of the weather we
took our shoes off religiously
and put tender feet on the new grass.
And even when it came late frost
or chilling rain we never put them on again
until the first of October.
I have walked with a stubbed toe
swollen and runny as a rotten potato
in the dew that gives blood poisoning
to turn the cows out.
By June I ran on callous sandals
down the gravel road
and teased copperheads among the weeds
looking for berries.
A tourist lady once paid a quarter
for her kids to see me skip
along the rocks.

I have gone barefoot into the creek
and into the snakey thicket above the falls.
Loitering discalced along the platform
of the market I stepped on
a burning cigarette, and stood
with naked soles on the hot pavement
before the courthouse.
My heels have been tarred by runny
highways and stuck to manure
and wormy mud. I have worn
socks of sweat and dust in the cornfields
and wiggled my insteps into the cool
underdirt for comfort.
I have stepped on nails and
barbed wire and glass in the leaves,
and stood vulnerable in the presence
of tetanus and hookworm.
Nettles plowed into the baulk
have left arrows in my arch.
I have put a toe in mousetraps in
dark corners of the attic.

The first warm day in April patches
swollen by the sun tear
from the pond floor where they've stuck
all winter coating the mud and rear
to the surface like leaves bucking
and shedding silt. Gather in thick

huddles downwind black as grease and clotting
against the leeshore. Under
the slick every drop is busy
as time's square. I saunter along
the rim and slaughter of last year's
cattails, feel the unknotting

and polymering amorphous as graphite
cells, surprised as a child
finding rabbit eggs in weeds at
the old impossible blessedness
in the royalling water where fish seeds
wink like new genes in the sky.

Concert

When Aunt Wessie played she
reached into the keys with heavy
arms as though rooting tomato
slips, sinking hands in to

the wrists and raking the dirt
smooth, humming as she worked.
Would awaken suddenly from her reverie
and plunge onto the keyboard jamming the

pedal in like an accelerator
and slapping chords over
the melody till
the whole room filled

and beat like a sounding board
and every note on the trellis of wires blurred.
Almost blind, she stayed alone
in her house on the mountain

while we worked off in the fields.
As her hearing failed
the TV blasted soap tragedy
all over the valley.

Too wild or many to use the coop
behind his house my uncle's chickens
gathered near sundown close
to an old arborvitae,
still pecking, a few
maybe dusting in the potholes
on the bank.
One by one they'd flap
up into the branches until
the yard was empty and
the waterpans full
of evening sky.
Squawking over favorite
perches and jarring
limbs they shifted like
berries of an abacus on the tiers
of hierarchy,
rooster high in the steeple.
They loaded that old tree
of life miserably,
thirty or forty
whitewashing the trunk
and lower limbs, dripping
even on each other.
The bark they polished
dusty with mites, leafage threadbare.

They settle into dusk clucking;
one flutters down for a last
blade or worm and then back—
disturbing neighbors to
reassert preference.
Frightened by a dog or
possum in the night they
raise a half-hour fuss.
The rooster crows by three.
Sometimes a hen gets heated in her
dream and lets an egg
go, bursting on the limbs
or ground like too-ripe fruit.
The fox may lick its
splatter,
but cannot climb.

My grandfather would say the arctic
camphor breathed on the mountains
that day dry-rotting flesh.
Back in the '90s whilom. He
drove a team down the frozen
creek to mill and saw where Searcy's
cabin burned the night before.
No snow, but scraps
of ground raised on silver
hair as if pulled out by
the near vacuum.
As if something big had left,
the valley ached with stillness.
The wheel was locked
by its beard to the creek.
Stopping by Orr's at noon he heard
the chickens never left the roost
but stayed on their perches like hoot owls
through the gloomy morning.
The callous sky and hungry air
drained his muscles
on the steep trail.
The buckets had welded to
the floors of stalls.
A wide absence drew from the ground
and chimneys every calorie, reached
into burrows and up the deep
hollows where deer
huddled in their yards.
The churchbell cracked and
bulbs in furrows detonated at the core.
The spring shrank under a shield
protecting its sources.
The parasitic emptiness
fed at crevices in rocks
and cabins. Such
poverty of the elements
and the splintering failure of
the poplars by the creek
took away speech where they
tightened to the fireplace.

Frost crawled on their backs
threatening to bite.
They prayed for the black
panther night to be lifted. One
asked to see the trapdoor of hell
opened as less painful
than flesh setting like tallow.
White spores cultured inside the windows.

Now the great warriors are recumbent in weeds
or moulder down the hollow
in a seance of water.
The stumps have bled wet tables of sugar
for years drowning flies and yellow
jackets, foaming like tankards

in warm rain. The wide platforms
of the titans crack their
rings and blacken
though we still read their methuselan
circumference where
they scatter like bases of a game.

The children gather on the rims sucking
on the old incredibly extensive
root systems and spurting on the ancestral
sap three times faster than all
seed growth. They put out leaves
enormous and lush from skinny

stems and crowd each other
into starvation. For years these
hinterslopes and clear-cut pinnacles will
wash away and chap in rubble,
bandaged only by brush and weeds.
Until immigrants and the rare

hardy scions reforest and reshade
them, for all the setbacks straight,
though less tough
for lack of competition. Of
the graveyards of the giants no trace
except likeness in the young leafage.

Wading into the shallows my father
wore the rock like an apron
streaming creek water, choosing

among the polished spill of
rubble the right thickness every time
for a homewall, completing already in

his mind the puzzle these fragments
would compose, selecting as for a
quilt contrasting surfaces, quartz

and peppery granite, and heaving from
their cool sockets and settings to dry
stacked within reach of the wagon

like coins and chips of his stakes.
To raise back up the mountain they
broke from and shoulder them

in place like jewels of a mosaic
thrown on the turning seasons, a creekbed
he wrapped around the family.

Surveying

The new-sold mountain down by Willow
will have its facets cut
and polished by the dozer,
and through the transit lens new
lines will be shot
and inked right over

its saplings. They'll pin
acreage to the flanks
and triangulate the ledges,
ironing flat the edges
of the hollow nussing rank
swampland at the foot, within

sight of Refuge Baptist Church.
With one blow of his light
hammer
the tongues-speaking auctioneer
transforms to rubble. It's the sight
of the still-wooded ridge that hurts.

After Church

Coming out of the damp sanctuary
a permanence flared in the pine
grove, and ice signaled from the
dormer cliffs and from

the snow Lhasas on Pinnacle.
Even the black coverts of laurel
and bleached pastures said
something comforting. And the dead

fields welcomed me to their exposures
after the swaddling word. What
could be more everlasting
than chickens scratching the manure

pile and the cold catalog in the toilet?
The wilderness lunged widdershins
moting the sky's perfection
and sun fell nondenominationally at

nails feasting, as they had for
half a century,
on the wood of the
dilapidating fence corner.

The story went that once someone, an unbeliever,
looking into the clouds saw among the luminous
caravan of shapes and smokes, the usual sheep

and outcroppings of battlevapor, signals, choo-
choos, stretching fish, when suddenly in
one great chunk of the sky the Lamb himself,

the face of longhaired Jesus, looked sadly down
at him. Struck down on his way from that moment
he believed. Having a camera he snapped the

quickly dissolving icon. Advertized on radio
and at revivals that photo sold thousands. Looking
at the black and white you never found the image

at first, but when it came rushing out of the
wisps and puffs hardening into a perfect likeness
the recognition was beyond all expectation chilling.

For months I kept eyes ahead or to the ground out
of horror, feared looking back I would see
the Tiger clawing through eastern azure.

Was said around home nobody
lived in Dark Corner, just
near it. For us it was across
the ridge in South Carolina.
After dark with the wind right
you could tell somebody was making.
Strong as the fermenting shade
under an appletree
fumes came chimneying
through the gap in Painter
Mountain. Whole cornfields asweat
through an eye. What focus!
Not to mention sunlight gathered on the hillsides
by the flush of cornleaves, and ground water
freighting minerals taken by sucker
roots, long weeks of play
with hoe and cultivator before
the laying by; stalks stretching
exhilarate in the July night
till sun fills the cobs' teeth
with oil. No mention
of top cutting,
fodder pulling. Talk
of digestion in mash vats at the head
of the holler, sugar agitations,
transubstantiations, work
of bacterial excitements till
hot sweetness arrives. Comes the runoff
calling from the corruptions and burning
a ghost returned by the reflector
to a cool point. Manifests
heavy drops, pore
runny with lunar ink.

Back up under the summit line
where smoke is hid by haze
and updrafts lift
the mash smell a few
hundred yards out of state,
the lookout waits on the laurel ledge,
gun in lap to fire warning.
A rattler suns near, his crevice
high over the settlement.
Down there houses propped, a toilet
wades the creek on stilts. Man
here'll go down
on his daughter, god
damn her soul.

Uncle got sent up for moonshine,
did time in the Atlanta pen.
Long as water runs and corn grows green
and fire boils water I'll be making,
Judge, reckon on it, he said.
But something there broke him.
Rumor blamed the whippings. He
came back old, a new man.

Turpentine the Dog

Catch the stray dog hanging round,
that howls all night
and quaffs our eggs,
that chases the cows into the hedge
to scratch their udders and heat
the milk with adrenalin.

Drag him away down to the barn
and tie to the crib
while you soak a cob in turpentine.
Then lift the tail, undoing the line,
and jab
the vaporing nubbin up his ass. He tears

away and jerks as though
trying to swallow air
into his behind—
and yelping rolls in the cool vines
along the branch. With a holler
drags haunches over

the grass, and lights out again.
You'll hear him bellowing
from time to time across the valley,
a squeal coming when he
thrashes in the creek and water stings
the burn, and last on the horizon

as he dives for South Carolina;
he won't be back.
I've heard of dogs lived seven years
after a turpentine but never
showing near the place they got struck
with religion and spoke in tongues.

Flood

How much the rain outside my window
this morning looks like a loom
strung with electric
warps through which the robin
darts and returns wefting
a fabric of summer,
knitting roots and new
borders on leaves; he
unties knotted worms
from the selvage grass
letting the full cloth blow
away and soak out of sight even
as it's woven. Now,
staff and distaff, the
rainspider has thrown
his web over the sun.

Drops slide along the twigs of the shadbush,
shift and cohere, separate and
drop off. Line up at a joint
queuing to jump
like paratroopers;
the load of drops remains
constant till long after
the rain is over.

A green floating of scum
collects in eddies
of ditchwater,
almost the pure
snot of life itself,
digesting heat, boils
in pools structureless, a blur
previous to form.
Bits catch and wisp off rocks,
stream away bright
polymers, constructing
colossal molecules;
fills backwaters with
green sperm.

A whole cloud fails out
on the acreage of the summit
stampeding to ditches,
filling depressions and

mounting terraces, spins
trees loose as it comes
down collecting everything.
Water needles down

scratching the grooves,
sets farm ponds free and plows
open a beaver swamp.
The creek valley is defecated.

Bridges heave
bucking away, a herd of
logs crowds into the bend.
The creek fans out over the bottoms

and fences of stubble,
slowed by area, stands for
a few hours waiting to spray out
the slot in the valley's lower

end. By the foothills it
hardly stirs the river's pulse,
clouds the swamps lightly. Logs rot
in the first lake's backwaters.

Go far enough upriver to cut in
so the current runs out
to the field's upper edge.
After the gate's thrown, melt
from the glacier meadows
and runoff of the high lakes come
proving every turn and drop
of the ditch, turning
loose on the field and filling
each depression and trough to
the lower end. Starts
sweeping back generally
over the ground swamping the seedriddled

ridges and soaking down to subsoil.
Water treats the powdery loam
with a transfusion,
like the introduction of a hormone
flipping switches. Just
when the ground's full and
before it gets watersick or the
oxygen leached, the gate's
closed and the flooded
land drains up into the sun.

Where a sheet of water lay
on the field for two weeks,
weeds blacken as though electrocuted
up to the floodmark.

There is the stench of wires shorting
out, hair singed. Wind fuels
itself on the bubonic mud
of a battlefield. Poplar roots are sore.

Waterbruised stems and leaves
slicken, smuts take on
the bushes and scalded saplings.
Leaves of the wild cherry

whose roots lay under the clear
sheet of water
cure yellow and
fallout across the rubble.

Because the forests and absorbent turfs have
been stripped off, because we build
too close to the moving water,
we protect ourselves against all excess,
domesticating whole rivers and watersheds;

empty or near-empty reservoirs wait in the mountains
with gates open and weedgrown basins for
the heavy rains or thaws, reserves of
volume serving negatively like the spare tanks
a camel draws on far from the oasis.

The more regulation the more we fear
extremes and overflow, the sudden wash
down gully and branch spreading out over cultivation,
tearing chunks from the bank and eroding
new channels. Fronting the river from where it

disperses into the gulf running back up
the deltas and boll to the tributaries and up each
of them to the foothills, and sometimes within
sight of the mountains, you see along the bank
and often miles over the marshes

and forested floodplain the embankments, the
fortification running on the land like a swollen
vein now grown over with brush and saplings, already
assimilated by the terrain, raised along through the low
country like some chinese wall against the current

from the north, against invasion of the deadly
overplus and its gift of silt like blood on
the altar. Our ramparts let water run higher than the city
it cuts through, waves sloshing on walls and fish
nudging the shore overhead. How they wait miles away

from the current through dry autumns and cold
nights. And closer in another policy to impound
and preserve, the cobbled banks and bed, the masonry
and revetments to starve the river of sand for
gnawing its meanders. Seawalls of boulders and pilings

train the flow. How we stick to the bluffs and far
back elevations, leave the rich low-lying flatlands
to reeds and swampoaks, leave a buffer to
trap and stretch to exhaustion the rebelling channels,
thin and dissipate the lethal thrusts, dampen the

amplitude of snake dancing, pull taut the
oxbow tangles, wall off where water would insinuate,
ride herd on the curriculum.

The falls milks over the rim fusing
to a central core losing
weight all the way

down to the first ledge it
marks by flaring off. Welds
spewing from the boulders whitehot.

In the arclight wrestles, plunging
a deep root into the earth. And
still at the top water spreads thinning

to the edge and tears
off a sheet sliding over, striking
wings on a rock wading in the powder.

The new water fails flattening out to
smooth the cantankerous shoreline,
but sluices

and sprouts a cold two-pronged
thrust clearing out in a long
filament reeled by the sun.

At Fundy waves come in off the Atlantic
into a long bay that narrowing traps like
a funnel or loading chute
the sweeping weight
of the ocean crowding down
the shrinking corridor.

Waves forced to climb on the back of
waves are squeezed tall above
sea level and rammed through the closing fjord
as the separate currents and lunges
resolve into one great vector
riding victorious up the canyon

to a glassy peak at the bay's head and
holding siege while
the pyramid of arriving tides
weakens and the deep pulls back its support
leaving the assault to fall away
and slide off layer by layer down

the firth. Villages
constructed near this extreme
are stranded across miles
of the oozing tidelands.

Yes, impossible not to believe that if
we paddle against the muscular current far
enough, survive the fever and mosquitoes
of the marshes, the indians encamped on
bluffs, make the great portage past the falls
reaching foothills by late summer, living on
buffalo shot from the banks and waterfowl nesting
in the shallows, Yes, we'll enter the long
gorge curving back to the snowcaps, and
wrestling the clear thrust of creekwater,
come to the final branch and its ultimate
pool. Yes, we can get out there and carry
over the alpine meadows and thaw runlets of the
col across the Divide. There! Yes, just over
there the Great River of the West rises descending
with ease out onto the floodplain, and gathering
in one long sweep through savannahs, past orchards
and grape-heavy trees, brushes away snags
and sandbars to the open sea, and beyond
the tropical, scented, wisdom-lighted
islands of the welcoming orient. Yes.

Land
Diving

II

Little town by the river
I nail you up in my memory
for good luck far from home,
as an emblem
I pass under hardly
noticing you're so constant
and everyday
there in the crook of the French Broad's arm,
in the frog marshes.
And I like to pick up and play
with you, toss you around
trying to score
on the peg of meaning out
here in the vast and traveling
world.

Voice

Creating shadows and dopplers
of obstruction the
pine filters song from the wind,
slices music from the open
flow causing air
to reflect and refract against itself.
But a greater resonance is
made by tying off
a knot of its motion in an eddy,
a swirl inside the mouth of bottle or cave,
filling and inflating
the belly
neck and lips.
And the urn or skull,
egg or hollow tree, glows
with sound
though broken and empty.

Though it's no disgrace refusing
some things must be done.
And present accomplishment
is no guarantee
of future.
You must come close
as possible without touching
to prove brinksmanship, fly
from the sapling girdered tower
before the whole village, leaping with a scream
against the wall of fear, step onto
the white-hot floor
of emptiness
holding only to yourself.
You will know the pure isolation of fall.
The vines bound to your feet must not snag
on the scaffolding
or they will swing you crushing
into the frame and braces.
They must not break
or be an inch too long
or you will be smothered by
the swat of earth.
Yet the meaning is the closeness.
No stretching out your arms;
you must be jerked to a stop face against
the trampled dirt
by the carefully measured
bonds.
Only they can save you.

Plowing Snow Under

Mold has grown on the field overnight.
Time to crank up the tractor
and plow under
the yeast-rich slickness,
reversing the sheet of new white
topsoil thread by thread.
The pure insulation
is ripped off and crushed
under mud,
soaks in like the dirt's shadow,
crystals and crumbs
of white manure
smeared in
to buoy and shoot the ground
through with nitrogen.
Swelling the dough at thaw,
pushing up drifts of lush green.

Dark except strips of light through cracks.
Walls loaded with harness.
The floor is a rich
sprinkle of feed dirt.
Rats crackle behind the sacks.
Reaching into the meal bin
the musty sides smother, but deep in
the crushing is warm
as a banked fire.
Don't cough in the barrel.
The cottonseed meal's fine
as snuff.
Vats of bonemeal, laying mash, nubbins.
Sweet dust of molasses
in dairy feed.
Bags of mixes, shorts
and sweetfeed.
Dust cultures on glass.
Panes of light like aquariums.
A dirty china egg lies on the shelf.

Hogpen

In the pine woods, at the log
enclosure with a roof
over one corner,
you can get up close
to the grunting breather.
And he knows you're there, always
watching through a chink.
Suddenly whirls
his great weight
squealing to the other
side, for all his size quick
as a cat; stands
in mud plush.
Living out
our exile we come
with offerings
of scraps, bran.
Slopped over and gomming
his snout he's after
it so fast, snorkeling
under, coughing.
Licks the trough bare to
meal stuck in cracks,
clabber whitening
hoofpools.
Sun brews the
tincture, flies steaming.
A scree of cobs bleaches downhill
where canfuls of worms can
be dug every foot.
It's a good place to play on
a hot day, in the pines,
spice of needles,
resin swelling.
Play close to the slow
talker
panting behind the logs.
He listens, taking
an interest.
Stirs in the inner
chambers, blessing the hours.

To be caught in headlights walking
the dark road seeing with
feet and body
alone
and suddenly hit
by the flame thrower,
vision splintered and nailed.
You are naked to the light's interrogation,
awakened on the stage, photographed,
stunned like the deer.
Shadows stream away
pulling at your feet.
Someone flicks a cigarette
sparking fuse.
Your first thought is
to jump over the bank and hide.
Only pride keeps you walking ahead
fighting. And you are left
blinded,
stepping through walls
of dark rubble.

Pumpkin

By fall the vines have crawled out
twenty yards from the hill
coiling under weeds.
The great cloth leaves have shriveled
and fallen. No sign of a harvest.
No way to tell where the pumpkins are scattered
except wade into the briars and matted grass,
among hornet nests and snakes,
parting the brush
with a hoe. Or wait
a few weeks longer till the weeds dry
up, burned by frost,
and huge beacons
shine through
like planets submerged and rising.

Though it can live on water and air alone
the lichen is not ascetic,
goes where it can
find space.
Chalks off.
Flourishes on bark.
Is a family, not competitive.
Farms the rock itself and when it looks
like peeling paint and old maps
is most alive.
Munches the rock
and soils the bare clay
with its dead.
Until vegetation appears
and the luxuries of shade and decay.
Moves on to the open, the clean air.

Just the other day I thought
of you for the first time
in years, cousin, and of the
cabin they built in the pines
on the west side of Uncle Jim's
hill, the shack of unpainted
undressed boards raised
for you to die in the last
winter before the war. Horace
you read and coughed there afternoons
with sun coming red through the
pines and your one window. All
the talk was Germany.
The preacher bibled by
to prod you toward salvation,
and couples your age courting
would fill the house
Sunday afternoons, your
father heard off
praying in the thicket. You
skeptic, witty, in love
with the draining weeks
of reality, the family's
last peaceful roman.
Dogs came to howl outside
and you could turn to
look through the trees upriver
toward the Chimneys and across the
bottoms to our graveyard
where in a few months you
and everything else would be
the same except the war.

Hoping he'll get run over, go off
on his own and die out of sight,
you put it off, can let no one else
do the amputation.
One of his eyes is a half

opened oyster, the other has the glaze
of infinity. He's deaf, no sense
of direction, control
of bowels or bladder. Goes everyday
shitting on doorsteps, stops traffic.

Strokes have burned off acres
of memory, bridges washed out. He's no
longer yours, but knows and backs
crippled when you come to kill.
Follow hating him for cheating

you of grace through snakey fields,
chiggers, through goldenrod, sweating
for a good shot, but he's gone.
Like when he ruined trout pools
you'd spent half an hour approaching

by diving in and thrashing downstream.
The running and anger make it easy. Find
him trembling, treed for
once by you and by age.
The shot heals but does not assuage.

Squirrel. Shadow

He stops at the lake
to lift a dry leaf off the water.
Minnows warm at the earth's hearth.
A butterfly shivers
its drop of art nouveau over the weeds
and a squirrel runs casting its tail on the sky.
The old man walks through fields
overturning rocks and boards
looking for an entrance.
Today the turning leaves remind
him of a rattlesnake, a briar licks his hand.
The sun focuses directly at his face
harvesting
itself and trailing off,
throws heavy gangplanks across the hill.

Loosened with mattocks and chopped
from rootholds, the last stumps are
left to be dragged to the pyre.
Tough cloth of topsoil unstrung,

roots pulled unnerving
and ungristling the ground.
Poplar roots wet and fat as worms
entangle twists of sweet sassafras.

The intricate feeders shaggy with hair
are gathered by the yard;
and the dirt, unlaced and

unpinned, is free to be worked in
specific tropes and turnings,
escape downhill in a few years.

Frozen Lake

Cobwebs and chicken tracks appear
on the surface near shore, thin
scum growing to
the iris of the lake.
Begins clotting and clouding
the deep pupil. Gets
hold of the body and
locks in place bank to bank.
The lake is paved with dry crust. Its
cap fits like a stovelid over
the busy currents where
trout circulate
alert as the juice in a battery.
Springs throb in the mud down there
and leaves settle in beds. A
muskrat ascends its duct.

Wind scars the warped rink.
Edges thaw by day and no longer
matching grind the banks. Laminations
of melt and snow.
The shores calibrate
with shelves as the lake
drops under its load.
Wind sands and draws
screws of snow off into the woods.

Sometime in March sun picks the icelock.
Heavy lids are
raised on each section and
rubble herds onto the
leeshore. In the shallows grass
leans free. Deep water stands.

The ink cloud drifting
in the pond is
tiny catfish
swarming perpetually
out of shape shading
the mother.
She turns
and ties knots
in the shallows,
stirring the mess
of fry like
filings, stroking
in sweeps and
circles
until fed by their
movement through
pond scum the
particles
eventually
precipitate. On
these hot days they
camouflage her watch like
floating
moss, each strand
an image of herself.

A chunk of clay suddenly
breaks from the thawing
bank and rolling
over gravel is
embedded and
stamped with impressions
of weedstalks before
splashing into the
creek.
Lies in the clear
ripple like a brick
of pigment
dyeing a
plume downstream.
Smokes and dusts the
shoal-water,
its trail
widening to
cloud the whole
current where it slows
into a pool.
By noon the chunk
burns out,
scrubbed
small and fecal, hardly
noticeable among
the seed-bright rocks.

Steep shoals
pyramid in the west,
high groves and
sacred
burial ranges
piled like thunderheads,
flap one on the
other to
high haze,
ladder up to the
dam holding back sky.
The great wings
back
each other
up all the way
to the final gap.
Clear weather
files the nick
sharp as
a gunsight.
I mean to climb
up there,
over the hogbacks and
heavy buttresses,
knowing hollows
and marshes
of meander
separate the
rough topologies, to
sit at the tip
of the breaking
looking over.

Paradise's Fool

III

Say the hillside pasture is the foot
of a long ramp running up to the first
tier of the ziggurat
and the ridge beyond steepens
up to another
shelf and the mountain
glides up to a table,
and nothing beyond that but
blue chimneys sharp against it.
Think how far that nothing goes and how wide.
Its other side touches the Other
Side. Though it's just three
big steps down to here
where plowed ground and cropped
grass are separate by a fence.

Rising a step at a time out of the valley—
finding stirrups in the dirt
to swing up on,
choosing
the next in mid-step
with no pause, one foot
rolling onto the next. Fingers
root for a hold in moss,
leaves, the dirt at your face.
And always the top just above with
the eastern sky pure,
almost black in the afternoon.
Once up rest
as in a bunk or hayloft
against the skyeave and look down.
Nothing to do but go down
and you go,
banking on rocks
and rappelling off saplings,
lose altitude so fast ears close,
dropping, parachuting,
till the ground holds out
on all sides,
thickets and marshes to crawl through.

At the timberline trees compact
and twist to hold in their sap against emptiness.
Forests give way to thickets that give
way to arctic moss and above just
weather busting rock on the pile.
From here the climb's rough
as the phrenology of mountains to look out on.
Lofty shore I climb out of the deep
spruce and rest on a ledge in the heather.
Foamy heather in the sun.
Tatterdemalion coastline. Nothing
ahead but clouds breaking spray on the turret
rocks. Let me camp here in the surf shrubs,
near the island's polar coign.

Sometimes I feel the seethe and crackle
of ions swept off the sun
as solar wind,
brushing the heat wool
and spiraling up blizzards
that far out cool and fall, each
particle refinding
its mate in the platinum mud.
As a tree sends out limbs grubbing
and dirt's hungry for sun milk
through rot and leafmold,
mind too wants the slimy core
metals, whey and stink
of the smelter.
Wants the steel honey
of the blast furnace.
Eye climbs open and finds the sun
high over the river, the clear stuff
drifting all the way down to the sky sill.

Beans want to climb.
They lift themselves up
and feel around for something to hold to,
runners already kinked, constricting
on string or cornstalks, felted
to catch any surface.

But cucumbers prefer to spill
out of the ground and run down
hill holding leaves overhead.
Have the same inclination
as water,
to pour and keep going.
Aspire only to describe the terrain,
seek no skeleton.
So you train daily,
twisting the woolly runners on hemp.
Lifting and tying under armpits,
propping
so they stand
toward the azure they don't want.
And at the top fall over again, streaming
out kitetails, hunting the ground.

To live in the mountain high
as in an attic with
dormer windows
and balconies,
castellated ledges
looking out over the plain
inked green by the little
lost river hunting
a sandtrap to vanish in.
The cornfields and sheep
are descended to by
fitting hands and feet
like cogteeth in holes up and
down the cliff's sheer.
Cool in the rock,
wind this high
always freshing the recesses
and playing the tunneled
passages where
grain is heaped and
cisterns of water cool
under tribal paintings.
Images gathered like honey
and brought here. Cliffdwelling.

In the still
of early morning
smoke climbs
scandent
taking hold and
lifting high
on the coolness;
a few shifts
and twists
out of true
alignment but
raises like
a charmed snake
from the house
clinging
acrobatically
to altitude,
and jacking almost
straight plumbs
the upper air
still reaching,
touches
a current
that spreads it
over the valley.

The two big pines that planted the grove
below stood among hardwoods.
Their shade was a dank
yard, a briary
tent, drifted with tufts
of needles from the heights.
The voices in the towers became
an obsession.
Looking up one of the masts
radiating its spokes you
saw no further
than the first branches.
Limbs near the ground had fallen
but the stubs remained in the bark
or cores of the stubs pegging

the battlement-sized base.
Climb up them to the first limbs (a pop
warning how much weight to trust).
From there on it's mounting
a spiral ladder, brushing
aside to find the next hold.
A dry limb breaks
numbing the hands, sickens
bones. The trunk becomes
tree-sized, green leather bark.
A squirrel's nest stuffed in the forks.
Resined hands grip anything.
Already above the hardwoods, looking
out windows in the branches.
Swaying now up into
the christmastree top
and easing into a saddle of limbs
just under the tip. Body weight
makes the sway longer, like a metronome,
going far out over the other trees
and back, canter holding
the bristly reins
looking over the pines
to the pasture. The steed takes off
as wind returns
spilling its voice
around and below you.

Rice

The most fertile grain would be
amphibious, roots in dirt, stalks in water,
and leaves wicking the sun.
The charge of three dominions
rushes through the filaments hotter
by friction and interreference than a spree

of acids. Sugars coil in solution.
Mud bristles like a mind submerged
out of ego into reverie but full
sized and available
just under the loosening film and urged
by heat to sweat out an explosion

of seed, spraying pure carats. As if
land sunk and water risen flush with land
achieve critical mass.
Register the sun's vast
pressure by darkening leaves and
stretching stalks with the lift

of hydraulic cylinders. The short tined
feet heave in the sty of hotbeds
terraced around the hill like threads
of a screw rearing stychomythic
crops afloat, quick
as if hoisted in locks of time.

One direction, one line of reference,
is all you need to start from
to go anywhere.
And though we don't
the blue sliver
hears
and responds,
aligning with its desire,
to a wind more subtle
than motion. Nervous,
alert,
always remembering
to point home,
a clock with one instant.
Though unsteady as mercury
and constant
only in approximation,
it lays off the horizon, protracting
the possible.

Volunteer

Praise what survives
its season of domestication
and sprouts along the margin,
among next year's crop.

Aggressive species ignore
fences and the boundary lines
of rotation to emigrate.

Praise blooded varieties returning
to the wild.

Spontaneous replanting be praised. Let
self-sowers reverdure the earth.

Let every garden and tiergarten and
sunken eden leak
breeds that multiply
to the limits of resource.

Praise all escapes
and trailing shrubs, runners that
spill out of culture
and reseed themselves.

Let volunteers find accommodation.

Witch Hazel

After the failure of vegetation,
the leaves' ripening and fall of
seed, while the summer's
mail is whirled

against the moon like geese
and loaded high in thickets,
when the orchards are stripped
and cornfields stink

scatologically, find
along the forest margins
and creek banks this
small shrub that held back in

flowering time, hoarded its
best sap through the sixth-month
plenty and dog days, and
harvest luau,

waiting for the first cool
afternoons to
open its heat to the
older sun, visible

now to all bees for
orgies,
dipping black wands to find
honey, corrupting the

grammar of the seasons for
a mardi gras above the dank
and souring competition,
flicking seeds on snow.

Fall

Now rain strafes the morning hills
and trees spend their lucre
onto the sky—
the sewers of the field are opened.
When the storm hits into the maples
it would seem that great
tokamak the sun is molting for
the woods are light incarnate.
Yes I too, looking at the rubble,
believe we have passed
a hundred times through
the guts of earthworms and
bless those transformations.
Coming in I bring
a seasoned log to your fireplace.

Coming on a hill many stories
above the grasslands
and wastes of far reaching canals.
Rain and high wind have exposed
bits of pottery and brick
around the summit.
A wall corner shows. Digging,
fortresses filled with blowing
dirt raise battlements
built on the ruins of others
ancient to them.
And those walls rest
like successive stages of
etymology on foundations and
castellations of temple-brothels
over cellar libraries.
Peeling off a few more centuries finds
a mausoleum unsealed and robbed
before the body melted.
Shoveling through silt, lamina
of urns, weapons, after
a few thousand years to arrive
beyond assembling and restoration
at virgin soil, without clue,
no origin. There at the center
of the first hill just
sandstorms leveling and filling
all depressions, building ramps
up and over walls, and below that
nothing but mud where once
some river anointing
the steppes turned back to the sea,
and dust saying anathema.

Copse

What a crowding at the boundary
between field and wood, a thrusting
out between the shade and cultivated ground.
Shielded by trees from wind
and frost, yet open to the sun,
the margin fills with seedlings and every

gap between seedlings with weeds. Thin
sprays of ironweed, thistle lofts
and turrets. Fountains of sweetshrub
confront and oppose, and broomsedge silkens
up to the fence and beyond, flows
swirling through alcoves into the pines.

Here at its shoreline the field
trails eddies of rye clockwising off
into brush. There is a rush to fill
every matchbox of space. This is the roost
of fugitives, a stateline perfect
for getaways either direction, concealed.

Mice traffic from field to stash, give
moles their preference of laidby soil
under pokeweeds. Frontiers of rockpiles
and rotting stumps nest rattlers.
Because it cannot survive
mowing chicory thrives

here. And lanterned sumac reaches from behind
the first ranks putting out a sign.
Every bush and sapling jams
its limbs to the frontage, crams hoping
to get a view, plugs every chink
to the open along the fireline

where wild spills through like magma shot
from below and strewing ragweed into the rows.
Briars splash and throw out barricades,
cast fishing with tufts of hair over rabbit
trails, grapple. Cobs left by squirrels
blacken on the shelf where the plowing stops.

Take earth, the astigmatic
earth, its biases
and shifty poles.

Take askewness, the wobbles
and cycles that though
imperfect
engender and evolve through
orbits that resolve into orbits.

The slant
moderates and tempers,
gives privilege by turns,
extending summer
beyond capricorn and cancer,
strums the equatorial
belt, fattening the tropics.

Flatboat

I could go along with this:
making a page out of the woods wherever
we come out fronting the river.
Just throw together
a raft with walls, a tray
of timber that's available to carry
us out on the current with maybe
a hut in one corner,
its floor just above water,
and a long-poled keel made from
a wagonseat steering in the rear
around sandbars and keeping clear
of the big steamers' wash.
Just drifting, that's me, lost
and singing in the river night past
towns and ferrylandings, going by
unlighted farms— just the
swish of keel and crickets in
the meadows, and a lantern on
the pole to punch the rising mist.
And when the wide seedbox
of cattle and hogs and implements
gets all floated down that open
highway in the wilderness, why, tie up and sell
it by the cord, or dismantle
and burn, or just abandon.
I like to make things that can
be left like water where their use ends,
that saddle a river's back
and take us part-way cross continent.

The overly advantaged
remind me of the young birch
that planted by a seed floating
to rest on a stump
takes root in the damp

composting rings and sprouts
prodigious, drinking
even in dry weather from
its spongy mesa. Lifted free
of floor growth, above competing moss

and poison ivy, it gets a headstart
from the decaying reservoir
that puts it up among the older
trees in a decade and sends
long feeders and a tap

down through the capillaries of
spunk and rotten sheathing into
the base of its host.
The problem manifests when
the privileging pedestal

erodes from its grasp
and the young birch,
stranded three feet out of dirt,
must trust its full weight to
slender roots exposed above soil.

Their inner ears and sonar guidance
systems eaten by worms
whales sometimes run aground
or stun themselves colliding
on maneuvers.

Washed up and stranded
by low tide they pant and blow
among the breakers, crushed
out of water by their
own weight, bellies

cut by sand. Their
arctic insulation's so efficient
they broil from
body heat out of
refrigerating depth,

skin blistered by sunburn
and exposure.
In a few hours they
lie delirious with pneumonia,
great cocks extended in mud.

The outer flesh already stinks.
The mountains
swell in
mockery of tumescence
and often explode

flinging tons of offal down
the beach. Some lie
days in massy fever, unable to hear
the others sing
in the deep canyons, flit

and call from the hollows and steep
meadows, chirping
through forests of light, in
touch with all other herds
within maybe a thousand miles.

When a big one hits out there
on the plains of North Dakota they
stop and stand, let
their enemy the wind
do the marching,
let the thick moldy air get
lost and go in circles
dragging the drifts and coulees.
Old buffalo he won't
even try for a ditch or
rock to hide in the shade of,
just stands there in the mounting
snow like stonehenge chewing
hot cud belched
up from his stomachs
and smoldering steam
while his wool cakes with
sediments.
And sinks down to sleep in the warm
hill of himself while wind
deflected hunts
in canyons and silos overhead.

Ice Worm

That habits the puddled feoffments
on glaciers unlikely
as a forest fire in Antarctica or green
meadows on the moon. That segments

life in the transparent jeweled soil
pushing out each morning to feed in a pool
of melt on manna of pollen
and algae wind lays there. That
grazes and lazes in the sun-expanded lens

and living high in the white aeolian zone
fed by air itself at the focal point
of its crystal dish observes the agon
of hot star on the sugarfields and lakes joining

the sky. And leaves before dark freezes
the puddle reentering through its pore the
insulating dungeons
while the million-ply gloamy sleep
of ice keeps taking up its bed on the ozone
ledges and going down to sea.

To my northern humor release
comes late and goes early,
but comes when it does with such
strength everything catapults
into growth out of

taiga and muskeg. The air
fills with thirsty frenzy and glaring
packice breaks shelving
back onto itself toward the pole.
Revenant fowl

clutter tundra and shore.
The grass untelescoping bores
in roots as the permafrost sinks
out of reach. Whales crowd inky
inlets and gravel washed out

of the mountains to the south
gems the auriferous mud
when ice breaks its showcase.
Dirt heaves in labor.
The sun never sets on this brief empire

of creation compressed so small
every molecule's candescent and all
seasons rub hot like brushes
of a generator dusting and cutting
lines of force. Where

the magnetic fountain rears
I crowd my exhilarations
into a camera flash. Shunned
by the long deliberate year
I make these few midnights solar

and strike into the long night of need
a rank garden, an eden.

Paradise's Fool

In the appletree abloom at the field's
edge and the hummingbird's
nest of moss and plantdown,

in the canticles of the star maiden
and subtle
aesthetics of failure,

the severalty of tidelands, duff
of fencerows, word amulets, stench of traffic
in the electron, I

am paradise's fool.
See the grapery and mariculture, whole
alloys of people, singing plants,

nut groves and
the clitoris sharp as a phonograph needle
scoring circles of music.

Lo, worlds without beginning in
the spring's contact lens,
the haunted well and camphorwood.

Neither in surview nor sweet veld
do I escape the terror,
the presence of the comforter.